S0-CBE-885

Courtesy, THE HENRY FRANCIS DU PONT WINTERTHUR MUSEUM

Tin-glazed earthenware knife rest, 1-5/8" high, 3-5/8" long, of European origin, possibly Dutch. Date 1720-1760. Cat's eyes hollow, apparently once filled with glass or stone beads.

Knife Rests

VIRGINIA L. NEAS

PUBLISHED BY GLASSY MOUNTAIN PRESS

Pickens, South Carolina

Copyright © 1987 by Virginia L. Neas

This book, or any part thereof, may not be reproduced without the written con-
sent of the author except for the quotation of brief passages in criticism.

ISBN No. Hard Cover: 0-9617836-0-5
          Soft Cover: 0-9617836-1-3
Library of Congress Catalog Card No. 86-90691

Photography: Jim Sargent Photography
             Easley, South Carolina

Cover Design: Tammy Burke
              Easley, South Carolina

Additional copies of this book may be ordered from

        Glassy Mountain Press
        Route 1, Box 417-C
        Pickens, South Carolina 29671

        Hard Cover — $16.95
        Soft Cover — $11.95
        Plus $1.50 postage and handling

Printed by Faith Printing Company
Taylors, South Carolina 29687

DEDICATION

This book is dedicated with love to my husband, who always said, "Go ahead and buy it," and to my children, Caroline and Jim Neumann, Philip and Alene Neas, and Elizabeth Carver, none of whom had to be told what I wanted for Christmas, and who found many of the beautiful rests in this book. And to our son, David Neas, who helped in the search for much too short a time.

TABLE OF CONTENTS

AN INTRODUCTION
TO KNIFE RESTS

Knife rests have been an interest of mine for twenty years, ever since my mother-in-law gave me a 1910 cut glass rest which had been one of her wedding gifts. I had to ask what it was, but the second time I saw one, in an antique shop, I recognized it and bought it. The third rest was a Victorian silverplate rest with a granite bar, four thistles on top and an irresistible quaintness which my family described as ghastly. But I loved it, and from then on was caught up in the search for this beautiful little antique.

So different are they in their composition and form — some glass, some metal, some porcelain, to name just a few — that their variety is endless and fascinating. The artistry of some in glass and sterling shows gifted design by the artist/designer, and great skill by the craftsman who carried out that design. Others are simple, crude, ordinary. All were made for one purpose — to offer a bar to keep a greasy knife or fork off the table.

Large rests were used for the carving knife, and soon a second was added for the carving fork. Smaller ones were placed at individual places at the table. Some were designed to hold both knife and fork. Others matched the rest of the glassware on the table, and it is not unusual to find sets of six or twelve matching cut glass rests in a leather covered box.

Although the knife rest has been thought of as a Victorian era table accessory, there is no doubt that its origin sprang from table manners over a hundred years before. The first rests, I like to think, were crude pieces of wood, placed on the table to keep some of the grease from the carving or individual knives of the diners from fouling the tabletop. Table linens were rare except among the wealthy, and some housewife must have become very tired of washing the table, the grease-spotted coat sleeves and the elaborate cuffs which were popular in the 18th century.

Several antique scholars feel that the knife rest originated in Germany and France, then spread to England and from there to America as travel between the two countries became more widespread. They were used in the more affluent homes, though simple wire and wood ones

1

were used in the ordinary household. Now it would be difficult to find a country which has not at some time used them — a friend recently had lunch at a home where each guest was provided with a hand-carved ivory rest from Africa.

A knife rest pictured in the front of this book is identified by the Winterthur Museum, Winterthur, Delaware, as tin-glazed earthenware of European origin and dated 1720-1760. A Bow Pottery rest in Victoria and Albert Museum, London, is dated about 1760. G. Bernard Hughes, in his book *Small Antique Silverware,* published by Bramhall House, New York (1957), mentions the introduction of knife rests in 1760, and the same author in *Sheffield Silver Plate,* published by Praeger, New York (1970), lists knife rests in the 1839 catalog of Thomas Firth & Son, Sheffield, England. Though glass rests were probably made in the early nineteenth century, it was not until the Centennial Exhibition in Philadelphia in 1876 that the brilliant new cut glass, deeply cut and shining like diamonds, brought beautiful glass rests into the shops by the hundreds.

It is interesting to note that combinations of silverplated knife rests and napkin rings, and glass knife rests and salt dips, were designed in the late 1800's. A rod extending from the base of the napkin ring served as the rest for the knife, and some area on the glass salt dips included a bar for the knife rest. The salt dips could be at the ends of a bar, or a single salt dip placed in the center with a bar on either side for knife and fork.

The knife rest for individual place settings was a boon to early 19th-century housewives, who could afford to have but one knife for each guest. As each course was removed, the knife was left on a rest beside the plate until the next course was served.

Knife rests were made in abundance well through the 1920's, and in fact are still manufactured today. Early Sears, Roebuck and Montgomery Ward catalogs show simple glass and metal rests priced at $.40 and $.58 each, and a 1913 Wallenstein Mayer and Co. catalog shows cut glass rests at $.70 each and silverplated ones in pairs at $1.00.

Since most knife rests average 3½'' to 4½'' in length, I have not given the measurements of each rest. If there is a significant difference from this average, I have given the measurements. Although in the United States we tend to call the horizontal surface between the ends the ''bar,'' in England the terms ''axle'' or ''spoke'' are also used. The term ''carving dog'' is also an early name for the carving rest.

The book has been divided into sections for rests of different materials. I hope that this will help in identifying rests. The author welcomes any additional information or corrections that should be made. In this way a body of information about the subject can be accumulated, instead of the phrase ''and knife rests'' that represents the only mention of them in many books on silver and glass.

2

POTTERY AND PORCELAIN RESTS

The ceramic rests are the most interesting of all. They are not seen as often in antique shows and shops as are the glass and silver ones because of their age and rarity. Three unusual shapes were made in pottery in the 18th century — the flat bar, the open triangular bar, and a third, a raised platform which I have seen only in a book illustration.

Staffordshire and Spode made rests in the flat bar style, and in the Victoria and Albert Museum we saw a rest of this type in white pottery with a blue flower pattern with an uncertain attribution to Bow Pottery, dated about 1760. A Staffordshire pair in this design may be seen marked No. 11 in the picture section following.

In an antique shop in London we found a beautiful example of the open triangular bar rest. Of white pottery with blue flower design, the

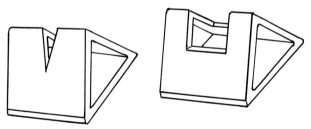

pair was dated late 1700 and measured 1-3/4'' by 1-3/4'' at the base and 1-1/2'' high. A ''V'' slot in the top of one and a square cut-out in the other accommodated the fork and knife. A similar set in the Ximenez-Fatio House, St. Augustine, Florida, is described as Staffordshire Pearlware, c. 1800, in white with blue decoration and gold edges. If you pass through this area and are a serious collector of knife rests, I know you would enjoy seeing this beautiful example.

In *Country Life Collection's Pocket Book of China*, G. Bernard Hughes, author, Hamlyn Publishing Group Limited, London, 1965, rev. 1977, is a drawing of a most unusual shape. It is best described as a shallow open-ended trough about 2-1/2'' wide and 3-1/2'' high, into which the knife was laid.

Among other manufacturers of ceramic rests were Wedgwood and Chelsea in England, Meissen in Germany, Delft in Holland and Royal Copenhagen in Denmark.

Rests by Dedham Pottery, which operated originally in Morrisville, Pennsylvania, as Chelsea Pottery, and then moved to Dedham, near Boston, were marked C.K.A.W. (Chelsea Keramic Art Works) in a cross formation. Dedham used animal and bird subjects for its crackle-glaze pottery, and a rabbit rest has been recorded in the late 1800's, with the rabbit's long, separated ears designed to hold the knife blade.

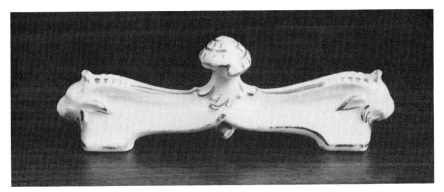

1. Royal Copenhagen, Denmark. White porcelain with gold decoration and lion heads on ends. Marked. Dated 1830-1845, though could be earlier.

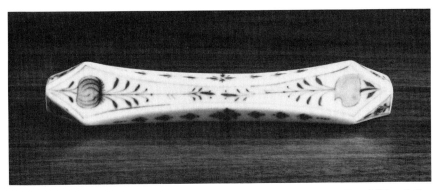

2. Meissen, Germany. Pattern called "Onion," "Pomegranate," and "Peach." Crossed swords mark. 18th century.

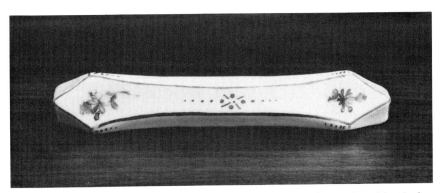

3. Meissen, Germany. White with gold trim and flower decoration. Identical in shape to above rest, but unmarked.

4. White porcelain bar, similar to oldest Bow rest in shape, but decoration of transfer-printed smiling cherub carrying a horn suggests late Victorian. Unmarked.

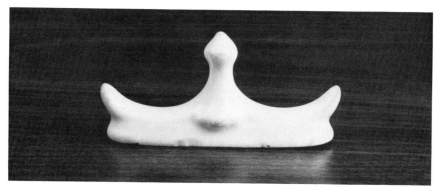

5. White pottery — double rest to accommodate both knife and fork. A similar design was made by Meissen. Unmarked.

6. Pottery with hand-painted figure of girl with flowers. Quimper mark — CX 794, France, HB for Hubaudiere-Bosquet. Quimper Factory in operation from 1600's to the present time.

7. Off-white soft-paste porcelain, hand painted with flowers and insects, high glaze. Unidentified.

8. Porcelain bar decorated with embossed bands and floral design in gold. Sterling silver balls form the ends.

7

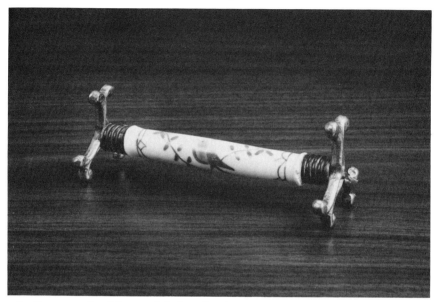

9. Pewter ends with porcelain bar, hand painted in flowers and bird decoration. Possibly Meissen.

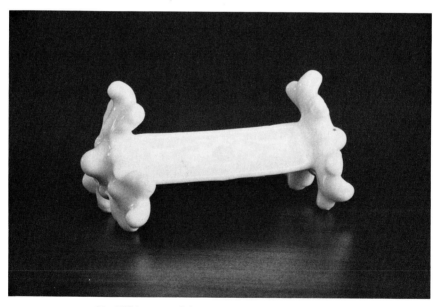

10. White porcelain rest — glazed. Unidentified.

11. Pair of Staffordshire rests, blue and white flowered design on oblong bars. Slight indentation where the knife blade would rest.

12. Blue oblong bar rests, glazed pottery. White ends have blue outline and red-brown design. 2" long, English.

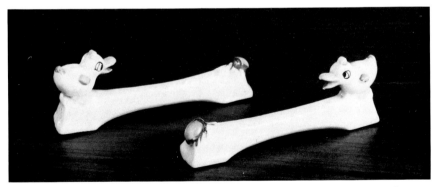

13. Pair of simple white pottery bars with ducks on one end and "June bugs" on the other. Glazed. Bought in England.

9

14. Unusual design. Reddish clay painted brown and decorated with flowers and geometric designs. Star on ends. May be from Austria or Switzerland.

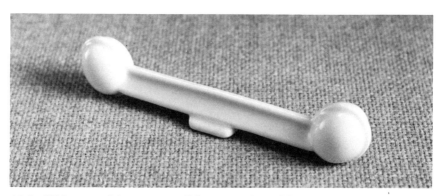

14-A. White porcelain rest — 4½" long. Egg-shaped balls on each end. Hollow. Marked "Germany" and symbol for Metzler and Orloff, Est. 1875.

14-B. Although this pair of rests was not marked, a matching mustard pot bore the mark "Sarreguemines, France (Lorraine)," Est. 1770. Hand decorated in dark blue with grapevines surrounding ends of bar, and drawings of a dragonfly, bees, and butterfly on the triangular ends.

RESTS IN SILVER
AND OTHER METALS

Sterling silver, Sheffield plate, silverplate, pewter, white metal, Britannia and brass have been used to make elegant knife rests. Both English and American catalogs show many varieties of these and those unmarked are difficult to trace to one country or the other. Apparently there was a great deal of commerce between the two countries in tableware, both silver and glass, and some borrowing of designs seems possible.

Two types of metal rests dominate: the jackstraw, with its many variations, its crossed end supports reminiscent of a child's set of jacks, and the figure-ended rests, with birds, sphinxes, animals and even human figures at each end of the bar.

Prices in 1870 for the lovely Victorian silverplated rests we search for today seem unbelievable. Reed and Barton priced the bar with birds on each end at $13.00 per dozen, $18.00 in gilt. (I have never found a gilt rest, but would like to.)

While these may be wholesale prices, even doubled they seem a tiny price for such beautiful additions to the dinner table.

A word about silver marks: I've tried very hard to trace them. Some marked rests I have been able to identify, but a dozen others have eluded me and some kind friends who also tried to find the makers. Where I could decipher part of a mark, a clue is given in the descriptive caption.

It would be interesting to know what influence the addition of attached rests to the carving knife and fork had on the diminished use of separate rests. From the early 1900's on, these sets were available in various styles, and surely eliminated the need for the separate carving rests.

A recent newspaper photograph shows a suggestion for a table setting for an Oriental dinner, with Victorian silverplated jackstraw knife rests holding chopsticks at each place, across the top of the setting. Perhaps their use will come back in the United States.

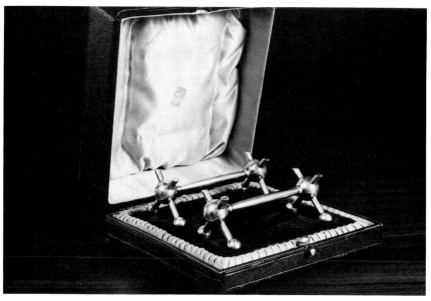

15. Presentation set of two silverplate master knife and fork rests in a leather box padded with blue satin. Unfortunately, the label has been removed.

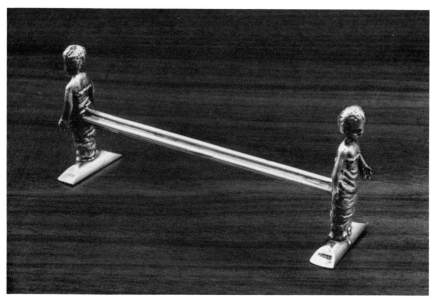

16. Silver. The figure seems to be a child in Roman or Greek robes. Marked Peruzzi — Firenze (Florence) on bases.

12

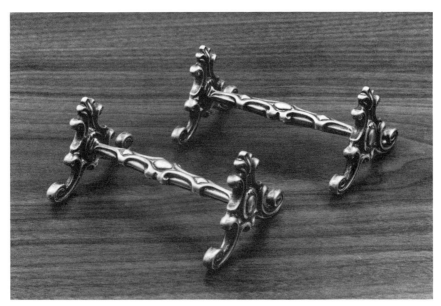

17. Pair of Baroque late Victorian silverplated rests, marked L JG AL EP.

18. Sterling silver, pierced ends with star in center. Marked George Angell, London, 1854.

19. Electroplated on nickel silver — lyre ends, flat bar.

20. Pair, silverplated on bases. Bought in England. Unmarked.

14

21. One of my favorites. Old English Plate. Two figures (soldier and possibly farmer) playing tug-of-war. Registry mark — date 1882. WH & SB, maker.

22. Jackstraw ends — silverplated, notched cut glass hexagonal bar.

23. Lovely sterling silver and mother-of-pearl rest. Art Deco period. Marked JD & S, Sheffield, 1920. Purchased in Dublin.

24. Four sterling silver balls hold a bar of carved bone. Ends of bar have decorative band in flowers and leaves. Ends slightly tilted outward.

25. Electroplate, mark unclear. English.

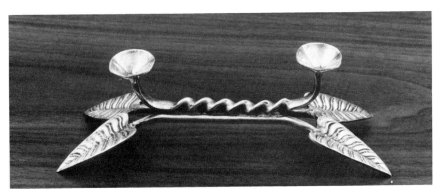

26. Late Victorian Art Nouveau, silverplated. Leaf and blossom motif.

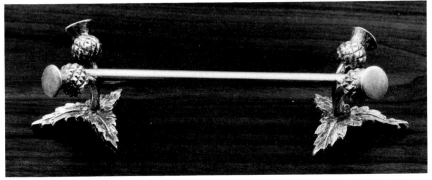

27. Silverplated rest, thistles and leaves on ends. Also seen with ivory or porcelain bar. Thistles suggest Scotland as source.

28. Dachshund, goat and rabbit seem to be the same type, but the little fox seems newer. Considerable wear indicating frequent use. Silverplate.

29. One of my earliest purchases and one of my favorites. The original price in 1968 was $2.89; today I would not part with it for any amount. Silverplate and agate, again with the Scottish thistle both in the wire support and flat base.

30. Silverplated wire, late Victorian. This kind of twisted wire was also used for picture frames, mirrors, and pen holders.

31. Silverplated, plain round bar. Marked Tiffany & Co., Makers, 10-J.

32. Silverplated on white metal and nickel silver. Birds spread wings on ends. In the Derby Silver Catalog of 1883. Other bird rests: one on round bases (also made in gold finish) Reed and Barton, 1878; another on spiral turned slender legs, Derby Silver, 1883 Catalog.

33. Pair of Art Nouveau rests in silverplate. Marked I/O OX 129 inside.

34. Large jack knife rest. Each arm measures 3″ tip to tip. English, late 19th century. Silverplate.

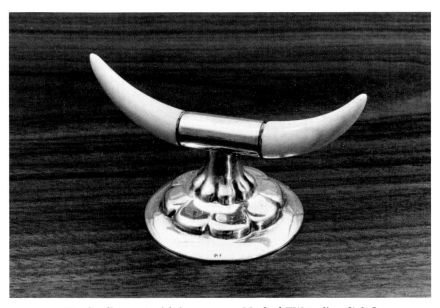

35. Sterling rest with ivory arms. Marked TW (pelican?) & S.

36. Silverplate — sphinx ends. Circa 1880. Egyptian design of the Renaissance Revival Period, 1870-1900. Reed and Barton 1878 Catalog. There was another sphinx rest shown in the 1895 Harrod's, London, Catalog. The elaborate wings are higher than the head.

37. Silverplate — jackstraw ends — cream-colored ivory bar.

38. Four circles enclosing fleur-de-lis on ends. Marked RYRIE.

39. Scrolls, garlands and flowers decorate the ends of this silverplated rest. About 1900.

40. Silverplated rest — marked Simpson, Hall, Miller & Co. USA. Quadruple plate. (Company merged with International Silver Company.) This company was in business from 1868-1899. The small rest, a child's toy, is soft white metal, 1'' long.

41. Wheel-like ends decorated with birds, insects and flowers. Art Nouveau period, white metal, silverplated.

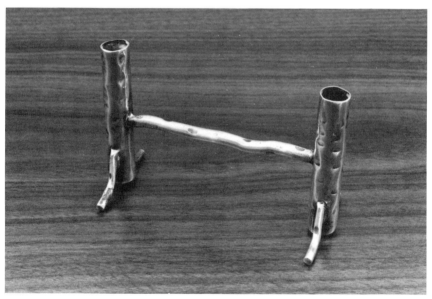

42. Unusual silverplated stile or jump for horseracing. Marked EPNS. End posts open at top. Some rests with the ends open at the top were used to hold flowers.

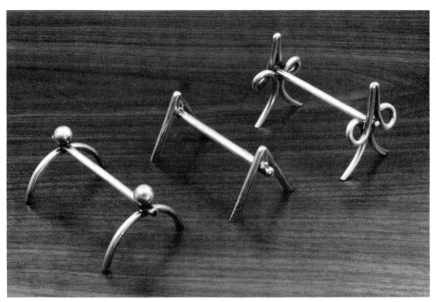

43. Silverplated wire rests. Inverted "V" rest is one of a pair. Late Victorian or Edwardian — 1900-1920. Rest at left bears badly worn mark, rest at right marked CNF & Co. 090.

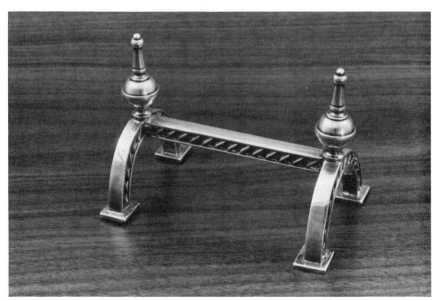

44. English classical design rest — gadroon trim on bar and ends. Maker W.H. and S.B. Marked February 21, 1872.

45. Rustic-looking silverplated rests, designed to look like tree branches, vines or bamboo.

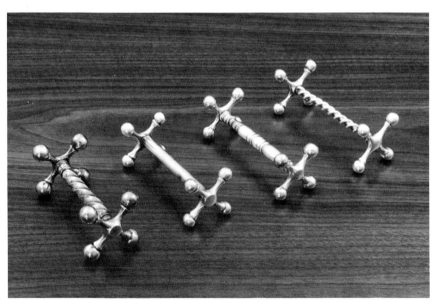

46. There were many variations on these jackstraw end rests. Each shown is slightly different in the bar design. The plain bar rest in the photograph is identical to one shown in the 1895 Harrod's Catalog, London.

26

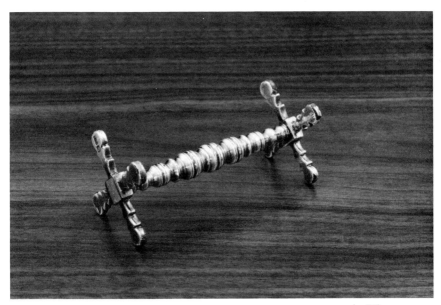

47. Old Sheffield Plate, made by J. Gilbert, 1812. Marked Gil bert.

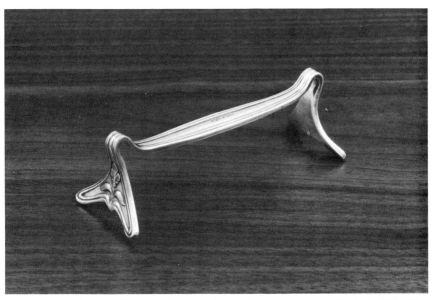

48. Nickel silver — silverplated rest of the Art Nouveau period. Marked AWL-FD-NS on top of bar, engraved initials E.F. in graceful curves on bottom of bar.

49. High crossed ends, bar and ends turned. Brass.

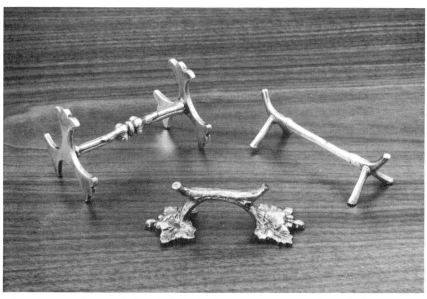

50. Three different styles, but all in the rustic or naturalistic design. Front: white metal or Brittania, 2″ long, grapes and leaves design. Right: Bamboo-like design, may be plated over brass. Left: silverplate.

28

51. White metal jackstraw rest — glass "striped" bar.

52. White metal or Brittania rest, jackstraw design. Bands engraved with flowers and leaves hold a six-sided ivory bar. About 1880.

53. Much used and abused rest — silverplated, six-sided bar. Squirrels in rings on ends.

54. Pair of silverplated cross-end rests, English. Simple design suggests Edwardian period. Mark J G A1 (Crown) EP.

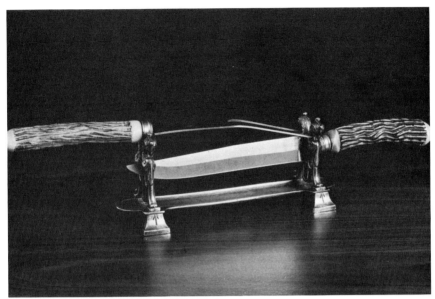

55. "Carver and Fork Rest." Marked: Manufactured and Plated by Reed and Barton. Pictured in 1878 Reed and Barton Catalog. Very rare, although it was a catalog item. Griffin heads on ends. Shallow, long drip tray. 7" by 3". Britannia metal and silverplated.

56. Silverplate. Scroll ends, hexagonal bar. Much wear. Shown in 1885 Harrod's Catalog.

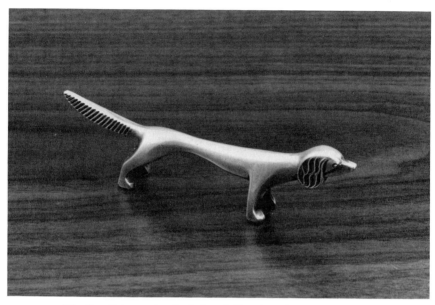

57. Swedish pewter dachshund. Purchased in Chicago area.

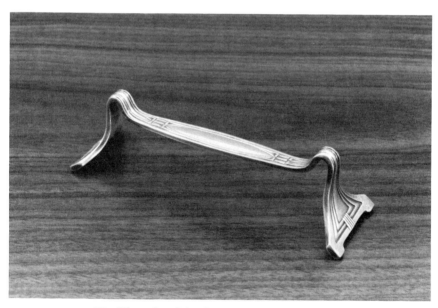

58. Silverplated Art Deco rest, 1920's or 1930's.

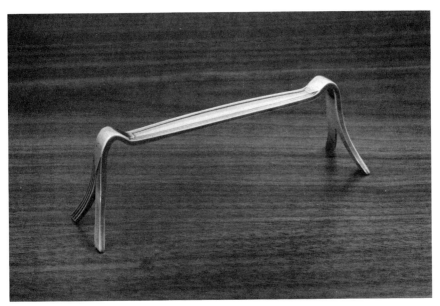

59. Art Deco rest, silverplated. Simple design suggests 1920-1930 period. Mark.

60. Silverplated rest, baroque-styled ends, slightly curved inward, twisted bar.

61. Butterfly-styled rest, twisted bar. Silverplate, Victorian.

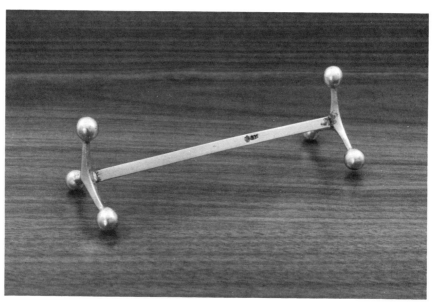

62. Triangular bar with mark (unreadable). Three-sided ends tipped with silver balls.

63. Very unusual master knife rest. Heavy brass bar and carefully fitted ends hold what appears to be a bone. This rest, bought in Door County, Wisconsin, has the name "E.C. Hall" scratched into one side.

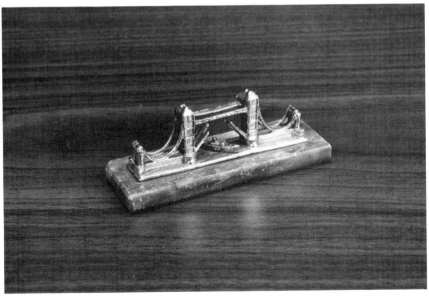

64. Miniature Tower Bridge. Silverplate, on marble base. Purchased in London — dealer's tag marked "Souvenir knife rest," c. 1910. A knife blade does fit in the top of the bridge.

RESTS IN CUT AND PRESSED GLASS

French writer Marcel Proust in *The Captive,* a volume in his series "Remembrance of Things Past" (Random House, 1929, renewed 1956, translated from the French by C.K. Scott Moncrieff and Terence Kilmartin) writes of "the hour when the shopkeepers go home to luncheon in the suburbs . . . in the darkened dining room, where the prismatic glass knife rests project a multicolored fire as beautiful as the windows of Chartres."

Truly beautiful are the thousands of cut glass rests made during the Brilliant Period, from 1850 to 1910, resembling jewels with which the Victorian hostess could adorn her table. Glass companies known to have made rests include Libbey, Lalique, Baccarat, Hawkes, Cambridge, New England Glass Company, Millersburg, Hoare and Company, and Boston and Sandwich Glass Company, whose 1874 catalog shows three cut crystal rests.

Hawkes and other glasshouses made knife rests in the same patterns as their other tableware and included patterns such as Lace Hobnail, Hobnail, Strawberry Diamond and Star and Hobnail. While most rests were 3-1/2" long, in the height of the Brilliant Period the size reached 8" to 9" for the master rests, and must have seemed enormous in comparison to other table appointments.

Less costly are the pressed glass rests, but some are quite beautiful and offer a large variety of design. Heisey, Westmoreland and Imperial made rests into the middle of the twentieth century.

The knife rest design which seems to bring forth the most nostalgic response in modern Americans is undoubtedly the "glass dumbbell," and almost everyone's grandmother "had one of those." Designs varied very little among companies except for a slightly different faceting of the cutting on the ball ends, and similar patterns in Marshall Field's 1911-1912 Catalog 178 marked "imported" are almost identical with those in the Libbey Catalog for 1893-1895. So these must have been made by glass companies on both sides of the ocean and were eagerly bought by housewives of that day.

Glassmakers in Stourbridge, England, made elegant rests containing millefiore canes soon after 1845, according to E.M. Elville in *Paperweights and other Glass Curiosities,* Spring Books, London, 1964. Rest No. 123 is an example of this kind of artistry, with a twisted cane in white and green (there are also other colors) laid in across the top of the bar. In addition they made rests using incrustations such as those used in paperweights, encasing a porcelain-like cameo of a bust, medallion or floral decoration in the glass of the object. These are definitely a prize to be searched for.

The maker of the "baby heads" knife rests is still unknown. One price guide attributes it to three makers: Lalique, Libbey, Baccarat and also mentions that it may be old pattern glass. One collector was told that the image was the head of Napoleon's son.

Colored glass was also produced during the 1800's and particularly the Victorian period and was used in knife rests. It was said that one piece of colored cut glass was made to every ten of clear crystal, making the colored rare and desirable to collectors.

A beautiful book, *Table Settings, Entertaining and Etiquette* by Patricia Easterbrook Roberts, Crown Publishers, published 1977, contains two photographs of table settings showing knife rests and several mentions of them in the text material. The photographs show the knife placed in position on a simple crystal rest at the beginning of the meal.

65. The first knife rest in my collection, given to me by my husband's mother, who received it as a wedding gift in 1910. Lapidary cut.

66. Cut glass — notched bar. Oval sections of fine cut and large oval stars alternating on ends.

67. Cut and pressed glass — tapered ends. 5-1/2''. Similar in design to one made by Heisey but longer.

68. Cut glass "notched prism" design. Smaller rest, 3-1/2", larger 4-1/2". Date about 1900-1910. American.

69. Cut glass double rest to accommodate both knife and fork. English. Fine cut ends, fine cut in diamonds on center of bar.

70. Pair of cut glass rests, notched bars, ends cut to four flat surfaces, each cut with a star. English.

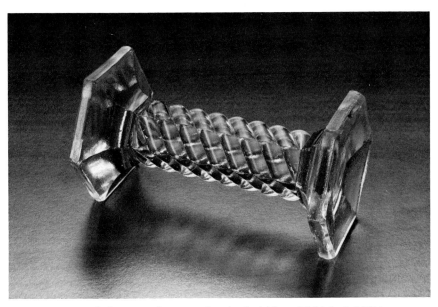

71. Pressed glass rest, hexagonal ends. Swirl bar. 2'' high, 3-1/2'' long.

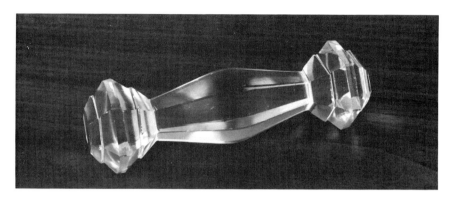

72. Cut glass. Bulbous center bar.

73. Cut glass, hexagonal ends. Bar cut in large facets. Similar in design to a Westmoreland catalog design of 1924.

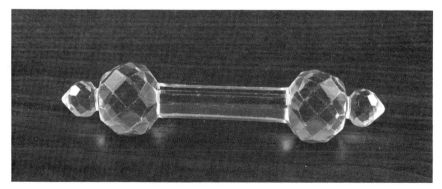

74. Cut glass rest — 5-1/2" long. Lapidary cut large ends with an added pointed decorative tip.

42

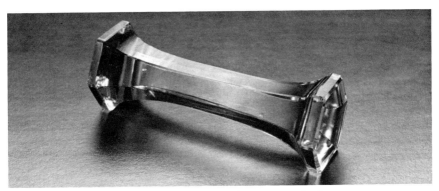

75. Cut glass — bar tapered to meet end of rest.

76. Cut glass pair. Notched bar — cane cut on ends with large stars on outside of ends.

77. Column-type rest, pressed glass, square bar divided into four sections. Large beaded edge on ends.

78. Three sizes, 6-1/2", 4-1/4", and 3-1/8", of the "dumbell" type rest. All lapidary cut, the largest slightly pointed on ends. The smallest were individual rests, and the largest, with notched bar, was for the carving knife. Medium-size rest — possibly Pitkins and Brooks.

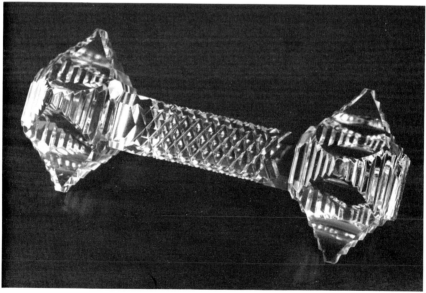

79. Massive rest, 5-1/2" long, 1-3/4" high. Rare shape, beautiful step or prism cut on ends ending in four points. Crosshatching on bar. Also made in small size, 3-1/2" long.

80. Column-type rest, pressed glass.

81. Cambridge glass, pressed, Marjorie Pattern, 5″ long. Large hobstars and fan design on ends. Made to match glassware service in late Depression glass period. A smaller version in clear plastic is available — I found one in a "bargain" bin for ten cents marked "Made in Hong Kong." Smaller, crude copies marked IG (Imperial Glass) found in 1980 in clear and yellow.

82. Pressed glass, triangular bar and ends.

45

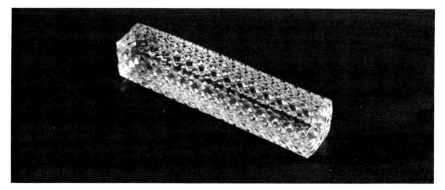

83. Cut glass, crosshatching on bar, star on ends. May be Pairpoint.

84. Cut glass, large faceted ends.

85. Column-type, pressed glass. Whorl design on ends.

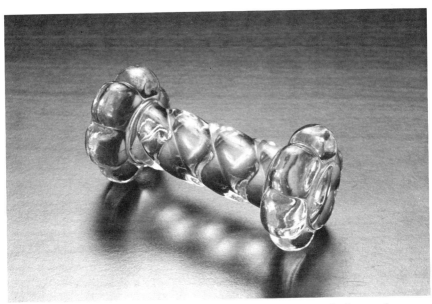

86. "Daisy" ends, spiral bar. Pressed glass. "F" scratched on end.

87. Facet-cut glass on ends, bar shaped to flow into ends.

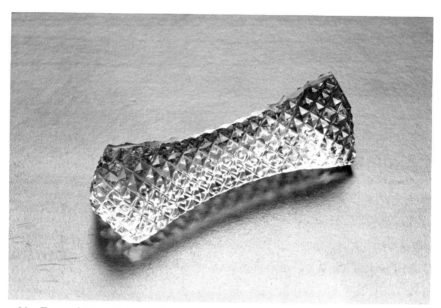

88. Tapered triangular rest, shaped to curve larger at ends. Crosshatch cut. 3″ long.

89. Triangular bar and decorated ends, pressed glass.

90. Pressed clear and frosted glass, "baby heads" on ends.

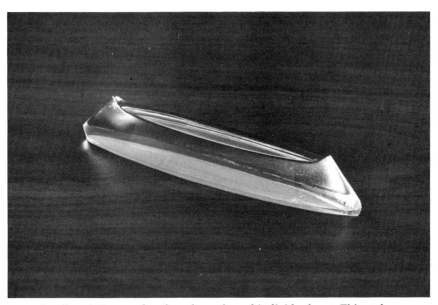

91. Small 3-3/4" pressed and cut boat-shaped individual rest. This style seems to be French.

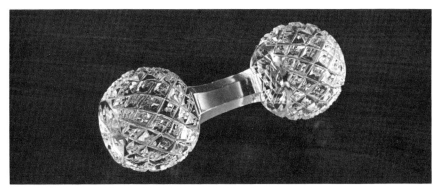

92. Elegant brilliant strawberry-diamond cut glass ends, bearing large stars. Six-sided bar.

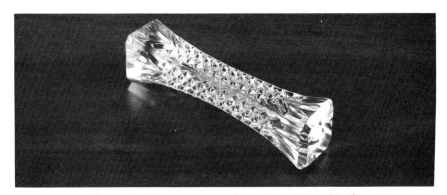

93. Diamond-point cut rest curving outward at end in fan cut.

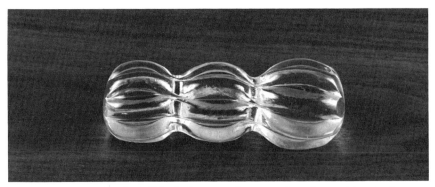

94. Unusual pulled ribbed glass rest, bottom of sections acid-etched.

50

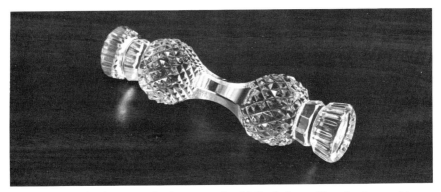

95. Diamond-point cut and mitre-cut ends, thistle design, with a short curved bar.

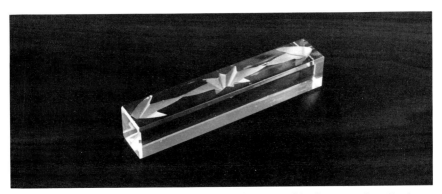

96. Cut glass bar — deep cut and etched in flower and leaf pattern described as "Italian Intaglio" cut. 3" long, 1/2" high.

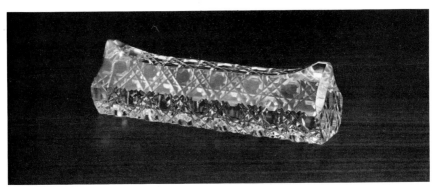

97. Cut glass rest — heavy bar with cane cut design on sides, and hollowed depression in clear glass top.

51

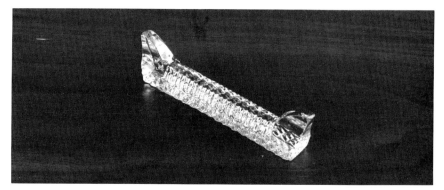

98. Finely cut bar with raised ends — 2-3/4'' by 3/4''. Individual rest.

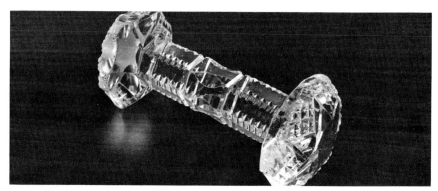

99. Six-sided ends are decorated with a large cut star, surrounded by diamond-point cutting. Bar is notched at ends, oval facets on center of bar. (See Rest #119 in color.)

100. Pressed glass bars decorated with fine ''cut'' rim on ends.

52

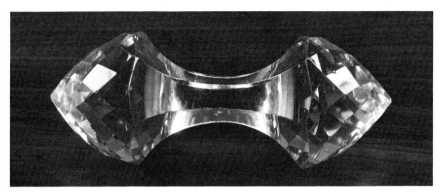

101. Unusually large variation on the "dumbell" style in lapidary cut glass. 5-1/2" long, 2" high.

102. Strawberry-diamond cut — undecorated ends. Similar to #92, but has cut and etched bar.

103. This pressed glass rest has a double mark — H in a diamond on bar and on end, made by Heisey Glass. Found in 1913 Heisey Catalog #75. Double marking was a production error.

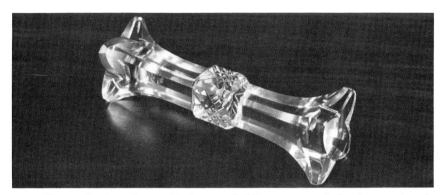

104. Unusually shaped rest with four petaled flowers on ends, knob on center of bar finely cut.

105. Beautifully cut fan-shaped sections alternate with fine-cut triangles on ends. Cut star on outside of ends.

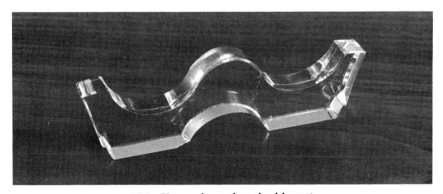

106. Unusual cut glass double rest.

107. Large version of cane-cut pair in #76, except for cutting on bar. 4-1/2" long.

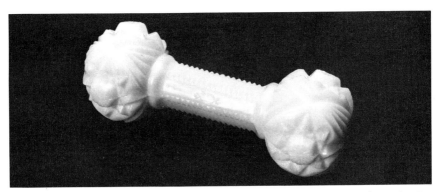

108. Milk glass rest — marked IG — Imperial Glass. Mark was used starting in about 1962. Hobstar design on ends.

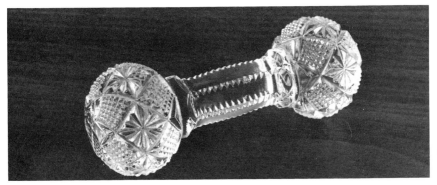

109. Pressed glass rest alternating squares of fine "cut" and stars with star design on ends. Westmoreland Glass, 1924 Catalog. A similar rest found in 1905 Butler Bros. Catalog sold for 84¢ per half dozen to the box, labeled "Lotus" pattern.

110. Pressed glass, clear and frosted alternating grooves in crossbar and around ends. Bought in England.

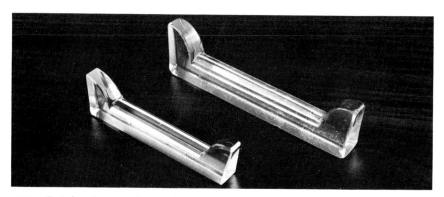

111. Cut glass bars, ends tapering upward. The smaller is 2-3/4'' — larger 3-1/2''.

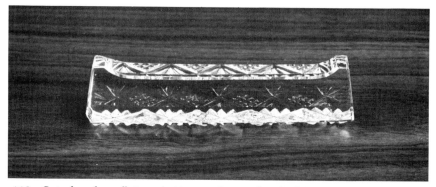

112. Cut glass bar, flat on bottom and cross-hatched in diamonds, with fan design in between. Clear top and sides. Seen in blue and clear.

113. Unremarkable pair of old pressed glass rests, showing much wear. One end of each has a round indentation. Included only because I like to remember the dusty little old shop in Tipperary, Ireland, where I found them.

114. Small cut glass fish — 3-1/8" by 1" high. Diamond cut. One of a set of six rests.

57

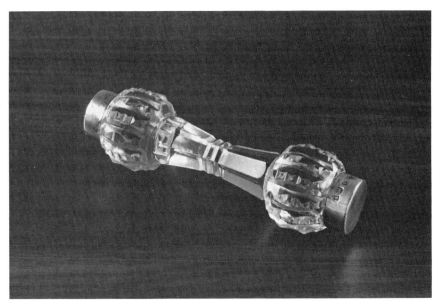

115. Small cut glass "dumbell" rest with notched prism ends and cutting on bar. Sterling silver caps on ends. England. Mark: JS & S.

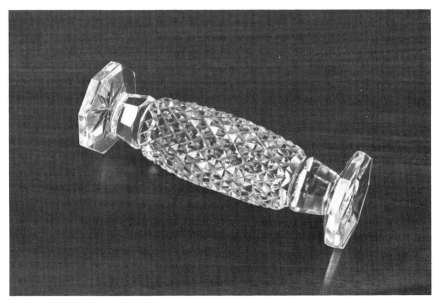

116. Octagonal ends on thick center bar — diamond point cutting on bar. Star cut on outer ends.

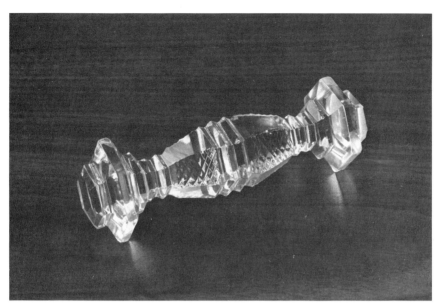

117. Heavy pressed and cut rest — cross-hatched bar. Hexagonal ends, step-cut.

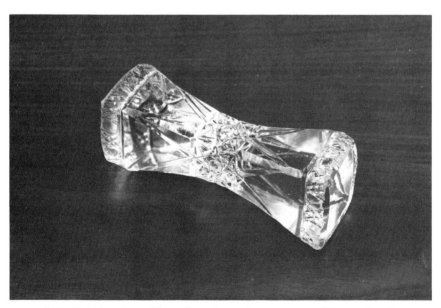

118. Cut glass bar, pillow-shaped, cutting on center of bar and ends.

119. Rose (or amber) cut rest. Six-sided star ends, alternating diamond-point cutting with star points. English.

120. Light blue cut glass double rest. Honeycomb cut narrowing to round ends. English.

121. Delicate cut and blown bar. Amethyst end knobs — clear bar. Said to be one of eight — each rest a different color.

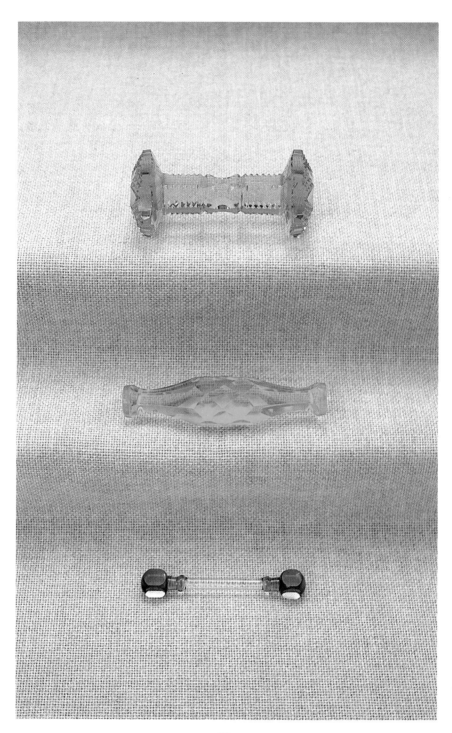

122. Rare cut glass rest in "peach" color. Straight square bar with beveled edges, a salt dip at each end with cross-cut bowls, scalloped top rim.

123. Clear glass rest with green and white cane across top of bar. Stourbridge, England, glass makers soon after 1845 were said to have made many glass table accessories, including knife rests, using a colored "cane," such as those used in paperweights, across the top. I believe this is their handiwork.

124. Rose cut and pressed glass, hexagonal bar and ends, step-cut.

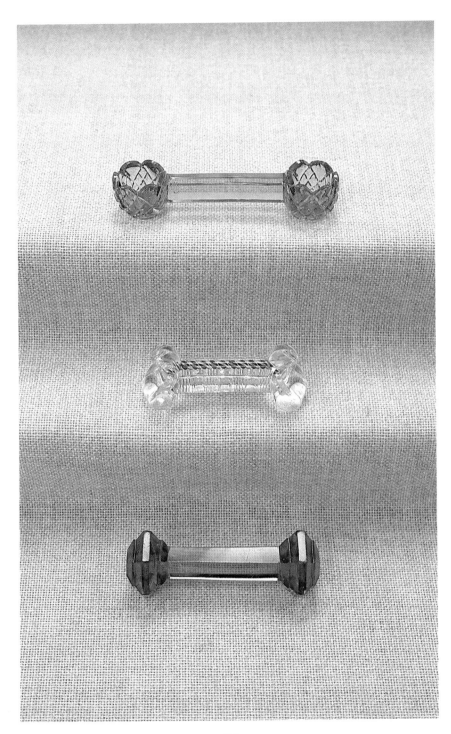

125. Large cobalt blue double rest. Pontil mark on end. 5-1/4" long, 1-1/4" high. English. This and others of this type were called "roll" rests.

126. Cranberry double rest. Pontil mark on end. English.

127. Yellow pressed glass, column type, sold to me as Sandwich glass, but not identified as such by the Sandwich Museum.

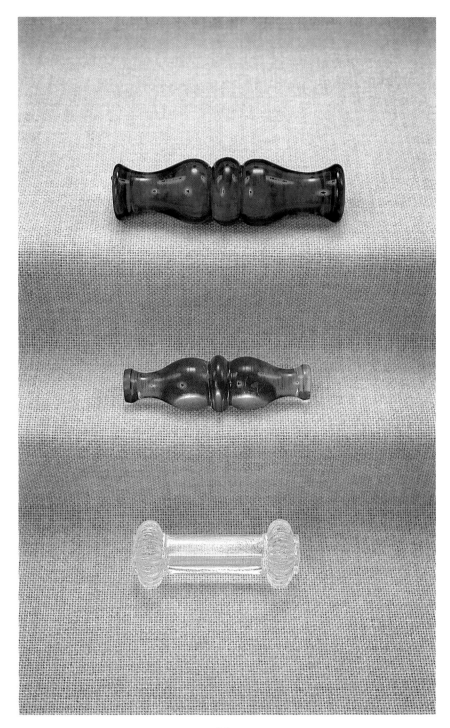

128. Amber rest similar to #120.

129. Green pressed and cut rest — six-sided ends and bar. English.

130. Amber bar rest. Cut design, fine-cut and fan. English.

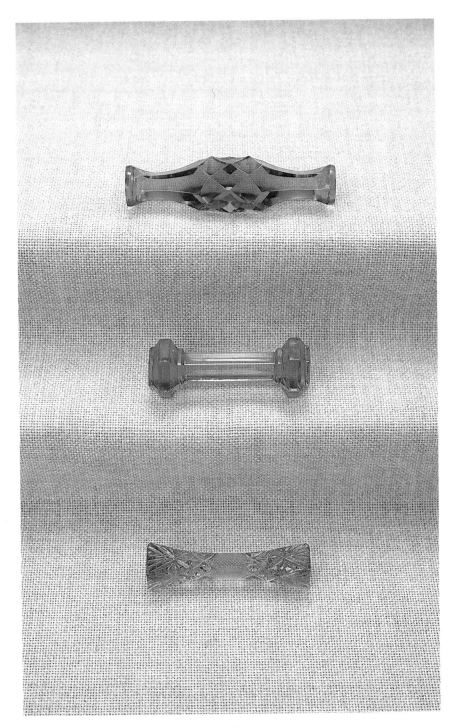

CONTEMPORARY RESTS

A surprising number of rests are being made at the present time in this country (these seem to be mostly reproductions of old rests), and in Germany, Ireland, France, Switzerland, England, Belgium, Taiwan and Hong Kong. Every kind of material is represented in the new rests.

Available mostly in gift stores, the new rests are often in the $3.00 to $5.00 range. Exceptions are the Waterford, Lalique and Sabino rests, which are shown in the following photographs and are in the $25.00 to $35.00 bracket. Craft shows occasionally are the source for unusual examples, and Oriental shops show many rests which are for chopsticks but could be used for knives.

Scandinavian shops come out with new designs now and then, and a current one is being manufactured in blue, violet, yellow and clear glass, and can be used as a candleholder, place marker, or knife rest (no. 152).

The cover of Marshall Field and Company's Spring Homemaker, 1985, shows a beautiful Art Deco table setting in black and white. At each place, holding a knife, is one of Lalique's contemporary frosted and clear knife rests.

131. Silverplated longhorn steer head — 4-1/2″ across the horns, 2-1/2″ high. Heavy base. Made by Gorham Silver Company. Purchased in 1978.

132. Though this rest looks very old, it was bought in 1967 in Florence, Italy, in the Lily Silver Shop in Piazza S. Croce as a sample rest. Design is taken from a torchholder design on the wall of Piazza Strozzi.

133. Pair of stainless steel rests, marked Sweden, Gense 18:8.

134. New — pair of fighting cocks. Pewter marked with crown and rose and the name "Étain D'Art," made in France.

135. Glazed porcelain triangular bar, gold decoration on bar sides and pink and yellow flower and green leaves decoration on ends. Mark Crown N, Dresden.

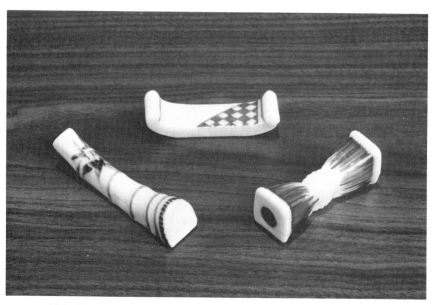

136. Three rests in blue and white Royal Copenhagen porcelain.

137. Blue and white flowered bar marked England. Sets of dinnerware in this pattern in blue and white and brown and white were made, marked "Calico," Burleigh, Staffordshire, England.

138. Enameled floral design on glazed red clay pottery, signed E. Georges. Possibly French.

139. One of four similar glazed pottery rests from France. Crude, inexpensive. This rest is sable brown; the others are dark brown, tan and dark green. 5/8'' high, 3-1/2'' long. Price — $1.50 each in 1985. Pattern is slightly different on each.

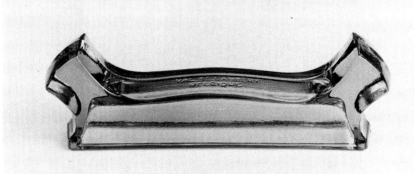

140. New molded rest, open on bottom, marked Val St. Lambert, Belgique, color — amber.

141. New pressed clear and frosted rest, etched mark Lalique, France, on flat base.

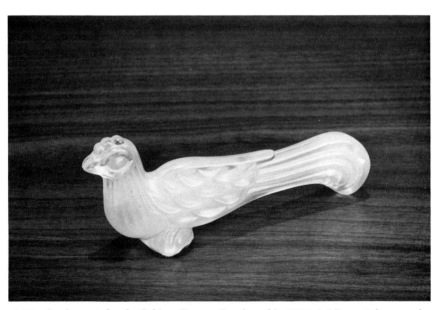

142. Opalescent glass by Sabino, France. Purchased in 1977. Art Deco style peacock. Other animal and bird rests were available in this gold opalescent glass.

143. Blown glass, white stripes on clear, flower end. Two tiny green legs hold this rest at an angle so that a flower can be placed inside. Used at individual place setting. Switzerland.

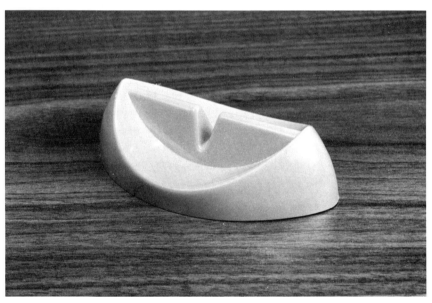

144. Tupperware. Olive green plastic. Bought at a Tupperware party in 1978. 3" long.

145. Simple wooden rest bought in Paris at a street stall in 1969.

146. Craft show creation — a loaf of pumpernickel bread with a slash on top for the knife. Marked: Viking Studio. 1-1/2'' by 3/4''.

77

147. Modern pressed and cut rest made by Waterford Glass, Ireland, 2-1/4'' long, 1-7/8'' high. A larger rest in the same design was manufactured until 1983, when it was discontinued, which could make it a collector's item.

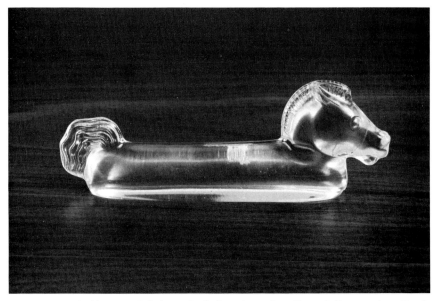

148. Horse knife rest. Label marked American Cut Crystal Corporation. Lead crystal, hand-made, made in France. 1978. Three other animals in set of four.

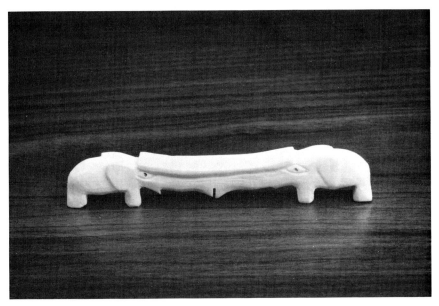

149. Two elephants support a bar for the rest on their trunks. Color — creamy-white. 4″ long.

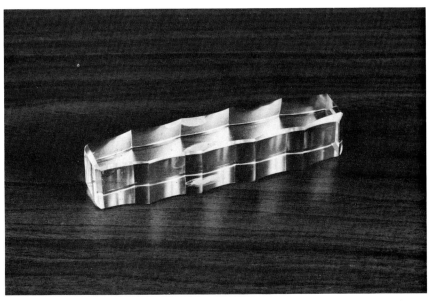

150. Cut glass bar marked "Made in Czechoslovakia." Purchased in Switzerland. Flat on top and bottom, cut on sides.

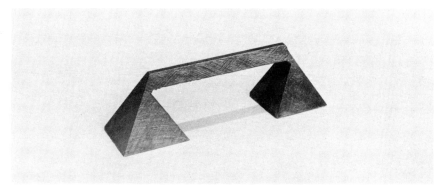

151. Walnut knife rest, 3'' long, made for me by my grandson, Eric Neumann, Christmas 1977.

152. Flower-shaped glass rest, designed to be used for a knife rest, place card holder, or holder for a slender candle. Sweden. 1985.

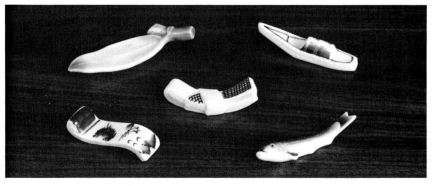

153. Five contemporary chopstick rests. Japan.

A WORD ABOUT PRICES

Preparing a price guide is a difficult task. The author has tried to reflect current prices from personal purchases and from other sources such as those seen in shows and antique shops. Geographical location and dealer make a difference in prices, and variations due to condition and age can be great. This guide is offered merely as a suggestion, and the author does not assume any responsibility for losses that may be incurred as a result of consulting this guide.

POTTERY AND PORCELAIN

No. in Text

1	Royal Copenhagen	$60.00
2	Meissen	30.00
6	Quimper	45.00
8	Porcelain Bar (Sterling)	50.00
9	Porcelain Bar (Pewter)	40.00
10	White Porcelain	25.00
11	Staffordshire Pair	60.00
14-A	White Bar	25.00
14-B	French White Pair	45.00

CUT GLASS

69	Double Rest	25.00
70	Pair Square Base	30.00
74	Double Ends	40.00
84	Large Cut	45.00
79	Large Lapidary Cut	40.00
92	Brilliant Cut	40.00
95	Thistle Ends	40.00
99	Star Ends	45.00
101	Lapidary Cut	45.00
105	Fan Cut	35.00
114	Cut Glass Fish	25.00
115	Cut, Silver End Caps (Sterling, Marked)	45.00

CONTEMPORARY

131	Bull Head Rest	30.00
133	Stainless Steel	10.00
134	Fighting Cocks	20.00
139	Pottery, Each	1.50
141	Lalique	37.00
142	Sabino	30.00
147	Waterford	26.00
148	Horse Head, France	10.00
152	Swedish Rosette	3.50

STERLING

23	Sterling and Mother-of-Pearl	55.00
18	Sterling (Marked)	60.00
35	Sterling, Ivory	55.00

SILVERPLATE

20	Pair, on Stands	30.00
21	Tug-of-War	45.00
27	Thistle Ends	30.00
28	Animals on End	15.00
36	Sphinx Ends	30.00
34	Large Jack	35.00
40	Larger Rest	30.00
46	Twisted Bar (left)	20.00
52	Ivory Bar	35.00
55	Double Rest (Rare)	45.00

PRESSED GLASS

89	Triangular Ends	15.00
90	Baby Heads	50.00
100	Pair Triangular Bar	25.00
103	Double Marked Heisey	40.00
108	Milk Glass	15.00
110	Clear and Frosted	15.00

PRICE RANGES (Single)

Pottery and Porcelain	20.00 to 60.00
Sterling	40.00 to 75.00
Silverplate	20.00 to 45.00
Cut Glass	25.00 to 50.00
Pressed Glass	15.00 to 35.00
Colored Glass	50% to 75% more than clear

ACKNOWLEDGEMENTS

I deeply appreciate all who have shared their knowledge about knife rests, Victorian silver, glass and porcelain with me, and extend thanks to:

Reed and Barton Silver Company, Taunton, Massachusetts, who not only answered my question, but sent copies of old catalog pages which enabled me to identify several rests.

International Silver Company, Meriden, Connecticut.

Victoria and Albert Museum, London.

British Museum, London.

Toledo Museum of Art, Toledo, Ohio.

Sandwich Glass Museum, Cape Cod, Massachusetts.

Winterthur Museum, Winterthur, Delaware.

Waterford Crystal, Inc., Subs. of Waterford Glass Group, Waterford Ireland, New York.

Mrs. John Rogers, Jacksonville, Florida, for information about the Ximenez-Fatio House, St. Augustine, Florida.

Betty and Remy Baker, owners of Schoolhouse Museum and Antiques, Liberty, South Carolina.

Mr. John Dyson, 27 The Terrace, London, England.

Fred W. Bickenheuser, author of *Tiffin Glassmasters,* Glassmaster Publications.

Carl U. Fauster, author of *Libbey Glass — Since 1918.*

L.A. Burman, Keeper of Decorative Arts, County Museums Department, Liverpool, England.

C. Parks, Corr. Secretary, American Cut Glass Association, Edmond, Oklahoma.

Dennis Gowan, The Spinning Wheel Antiques, Greenville, South Carolina.

Louise Bell, Seneca, South Carolina.

John and Sally Dittman, Easley, South Carolina, for their research at Sandwich Glass Museum.

Irene Taylor, who encouraged me from the beginning, and helped me
find many unique rests while she was working on her annual *Guide
to Antique Shops of Northern Illinois and Southern Wisconsin,* and to
Cecil Taylor, who found the Marcel Proust quotation.

Reference Staff of Pickens County Library, Easley, South Carolina.

Kathy Hughes, Tudor House Galleries, 2900 Selwyn Avenue, Charlotte,
North Carolina, who graciously loaned the rests numbered 79, 105,
115, and 125 so that I might include them in this book.

An article about some of my knife rests appeared in the *Antique
Trader,* January 28, 1983, written by Carolyn Dahlberg.

The kind people named below were thoughtful enough to write to me
and helped with information from their own collections. I knew there
were other collectors out there who got the rests the dealers told me they
had just sold!

Sheri Esposito, Wheaton, Illinois; Leslie B. Halpern, San Francisco;
Virginia Peterson, Tacoma, Washington; Alice Plasterer, Strasburg,
Pennsylvania; E. Lucille Higgs, Tallahassee, Florida; Dr. Robert
Schoenwetter, Oshkosh, Wisconsin; and Major John H. Rutledge,
Arlington, Virginia.

To Bob and Lory Mauney, Arlington Heights, Illinois, a special thanks
for our many days of antiquing together, which were for us the very best
of times.

And to Jim Sargent, our thanks for the many hours of work and great
care he has given to make the fine pictures in this book.

BIBLIOGRAPHY

Antiques Research Publications
Butler Brothers' Catalog, 1905. Reprint — Glassware, Mentone, Alabama.
Bentley, Nicolas
The Victorian Scene: 1837-1901, George Weidenfeld and Nicolson, London, 1968.
Boggess, Bill and Louise
American Brilliant Cut Glass, Crown Publishing, 1977.
Bradbury, Frederick
Bradbury's Book of Hallmarks, J.W. Northend, Ltd., Sheffield, England, 1982.
Brion, Marcel
The Medici, Crown, 1969.
Brown, Clark W.
Salt Dishes, Mid-America Book Co., 1968.
Carpenter, Charles H., Jr. and Mary
Tiffany Silver, Dodd, Mead, 1978.
Cohen, Hal L.
Official Guide to Silver and Silverplate, House of Collectibles, 1974.
Crawford, Tad
~~~~~~~~~~~~~ Guide, Hawthorn Books, 1977.

p. 85 The publication date
of Dorothy Daniel's book
should be 1950.

~~Antique Silver~~ ~~
Elville, E.M.
English and Irish Cut Glass 1750-1950, Country Life Limited, 1953.
Evers, Jo
The Standard Cut Glass Value Guide, Collector Books, 1975.
Fauster, Carl
Libbey Glass Since 1818, Len Beach Press, 1979.
Freeman, Dr. Larry
Early American Plated Silver, Century House, Watkins Glen, New

York, 1973.

Hobbies Magazine, August 1966.
> Article, Knife Rests, by Patricia and Jack Miscall, Lake Forest, Illinois.

Holland, Margaret
> *Phaidon Guide to Silver,* Prentice Hall, 1983.

Hotchkiss, John F.
> *Cut Glass Handbook and Price Guide,* John F. Hotchkiss, 1970, Wallace-Homestead.

Hughes, G. Bernard
> *The Country Life Collection's Pocket Book of China,* Hamlyn Publishing Group Limited, London, 1965. Rev. 1977.
> *Sheffield Silver Plate,* Praeger Publications, Inc., New York, 1970.

Kovel, Ralph M. and Terry H.
> *Dictionary of Marks, Pottery and Porcelain,* Crown, 1953.
> *Kovel's Complete Antiques Price List,* Rev. 7th Ed.
> *Know Your Antiques,* Crown Publishers, 1967.

Lee, Robert W.
> *Boston and Sandwich Glass Co. 1874 Catalog,* Lee Publishing, 1968.

Libbey Glass Co.
> *Cut Glass Catalog 1896,* Toledo, Ohio.

McClinton, Katherine Morrison
> *Collecting American 19th-Century Silver,* Charles Scribner's Sons, 1968.
> *Lalique for Collectors,* Charles Scribner's Sons, 1968.

Mebane, John
> *Poor Man's Guide to Antique Collecting,* Doubleday and Company, Inc., 1969.

Pearson, J. Michael and Dorothy T.
> *American Cut Glass for the Discriminating Collector,* Vantage Press, 1968.

Rainwater, Dorothy T. and H. Ivan
> *American Silverplate,* Thomas Nelson, Inc., and Everybody's Press, 1968.

Roberts, Patricia Easterbrook
> *Table Settings, Entertaining and Etiquette,* Bonanza Books, 1967.

Schnadig, Victor K.
> *American-Victorian Figural Napkin Rings,* Wallace-Homestead Book Co., 1971.

Victorian Silverplated Holloware
> Rogers Brothers Mfg. Co., 1857; Meriden Britannia Co., 1867; Derby Silver Co., 1883, Pyne Press, 1972.

Victorian Silverplated Holloware
    Wallace-Homestead.
Warman, Edwin G.
    American Cut Glass, Warman Publishing Co., 1957.
Wyler, Seymour B.
    The Book of Old Silver, Crown Publishing, 1937.